BARBAROSSA

BARBAROSSA

The German Invasion of the Soviet Union
and the Siege of Leningrad:

Sonnets

JONATHAN FINK

DZANC
BOOKS

DZANC BOOKS

5220 Dexter Ann Arbor Rd.
Ann Arbor, MI 48103
www.dzancbooks.org

Designed by Steven Seighman

Library of Congress Cataloging-in-Publication Data

Names: Fink, Jonathan, author. Title: Barbarossa : the German in-
vasion of the Soviet Union and the siege of   Leningrad : sonnets /
Jonathan Fink. Description: First edition. | Ann Arbor, MI : Dzanc
Books, 2016. Identifiers: LCCN 2016009532 | ISBN 9781941088555
(softcover) Subjects: | BISAC: POETRY / American / General.Clas-
sification: LCC PS3606.I545 A6 2016 | DDC 811/.6—dc23LC record
available at https://lccn.loc.gov/2016009532
ISBN: 978-1-941088-55-5

First U.S. Edition: November 2016

Printed in the United States of America

10 9 8 7 6 5 4 3 2 1

Contents

I. INVASION

III. THE BATTLE FOR LENINGRAD

IV. THE ICE ROAD

Acknowledgments

I am grateful to the National Endowment for the Arts for a Literature Fellowship that supported me in the undertaking of this project; the Summer Literary Seminars program for an invitation to serve as a lecturer in the St. Petersburg program; the Florida Division of Cultural Affairs for an Individual Artist's Fellowship that aided me in the completion of these poems; and the University of West Florida for travel and research support. Without the support of these groups, this project would not have been possible.

Several nonfiction books were also especially informative to my process: *The 900 Days: The Siege of Leningrad* by Harrison E. Salisbury, *Russia Besieged* by Nicholas Bethell, and *The Siege of Leningrad* by Leon Goure.

"The Air Raids," "To Protect Their Belongings, Some Leningraders Wear Their Finest Clothes," "In the Workshops," "Accusations," "The Battle for Leningrad Begins," and "Imitation" appeared in *The Common*. "Section IV: The Ice Road" originally appeared online as a standalone sequence at *Connotation Press: An Online Artifact*. "Bombs Fall Near a Zoo" appeared in *Crazyhorse*. "The Evacuation of Children from Leningrad" appeared in *Measure*.

Preface

Nearly two full years after Germany invaded Poland in 1939, Adolf Hitler and the German army showed no evidence of relenting in the Nazi expansion across Europe. France had fallen to Germany in the summer of 1940, and the heavy German bombing of London commenced less than a year later, in May. Hitler, believing he was able to devote his forces more fully to a two-front war, turned his attention to the Soviet Union in the summer of 1941. By mid-June, German forces had amassed along the western border of Russia. When the German operation "Barbarossa" began, the Soviet Union was poorly prepared for the invasion. Stalin, still trusting (whether from naiveté or out of political necessity) to the Russo-German alliance, initially refused to acknowledge the invasion, disregarding reports from the front and insisting that Soviet soldiers should not fire on Germans under any circumstance. The German invasion of the Soviet Union began on June 22, 1941. Over the next four years, Soviet civilians and soldiers would die from starvation, execution, battle, and illness. The total number of Soviet deaths in World War II is often cited between eighteen and twenty-five million.

In the Leningrad area alone, between 1.6 million and 2 million Soviet citizens perished from the summer of 1941 to the summer of 1944. The following sonnet sequence focuses on the first year of the siege—from the initial German invasion of the Soviet Union to the formation of supply routes over the frozen Lake Ladoga.

My visit to the Museum of the Defense and Siege of Leningrad crystallized my awareness of the collective and individual suffering experienced by the citizens of Leningrad. Over the course of this project, my aesthetic touchstone remained two small artifacts I observed in the museum: a three-panel sequence of photographic portraits of a young woman, and a display of a square of bread approximately the size of two fingers. The images of the woman revealed her aging over the nine hundred days of the siege from a woman in her early twenties to a woman skeletal and emaciated, her age virtually indecipherable. The bread—placed next to a knife on a wood cutting board in a recreated Leningrad apartment—represented the daily ration (125 grams) each citizen received at the height of the siege. My hope, through a similar distillation and compression of historical material through the form of the sonnet, is to engage the tension, complexity, and singularity of the individual lives of citizens, soldiers, and politicians transformed by the siege.

I. INVASION

Shelling Begins on the Russo-German Border

June 22, 1941—

a train pulls slowly from a station; wheels
bear down and shudder slightly as they turn.
The railroad tracks run by a road. The trill
of steam releasing in the air, the plume
of smoke, are commonplace, routine. A man
stops pedaling his bicycle. *The fumes*
of gasoline? he thinks and tilts his head.
A fire perhaps? He runs his fingers through
the coarseness of his hair, then wipes the fronts
and backs across his chest. The whistle grows
in pitch and volume—shrill, a bird. He grunts.
The birds become a flock, a drove. No wings.
No beaks. Just shadows diving. Steel that sings.

German Motorcyclists Surprise Russian Infantry Soldiers Still Undergoing Drill Instruction

At first, the motorcyclists must seem
to be a test to Russian soldiers, part
of drills and lessons, officers concealed
in stolen German uniforms, the sort
of detail calculated to unnerve.
Perhaps a German soldier wipes the grime
off from his goggles, pauses, and then turns
the throttle open, revving it one time,
the way he did when young, when he first pieced
together engines and then took them back
apart to learn their workings. Then he speaks,
the words unrecognizable. *A pack
of wolves,* one Russian soldier thinks, as men
in sidecars raise machineguns on command.

A Section of Horse-Drawn Field Artillery Crossing a Stream: Photograph

Three-headed beasts, the photograph so dark
the horses in each row must writhe as one,
their six legs caught in flight, as still as trunks
of trees—some straight, some curved—along the bank.
Three-headed beasts, like Cerberus, the Fates,
the Trinity, but here the steeds are none
of these—they shit and snort; they bow, in turn,
their three dark heads then raise them, straining, each
plunge of their necks a piston firing. Ears
pricked forward, ears pinned back, the horses race
because they're told to race. The viewer first
expects a gilded coach, a bride in tears
inside, whisked to or from a wedding, lace
veil pulling free as blessing or as curse.

General Dmitry Pavlov, at a Comedic Play in the Officers' Club in Minsk, Refuses to Believe the Invasion Has Begun

All great betrayals move in daylight, pass
like kin into the land on widest roads,
burn fields and crops and salt the earth, burn homes
to usher out the living. Nothing lasts.
And as the audience begins to laugh,
Dmitry waves away the news when told
of the invasion. Jesters tear the folds
of cloth a woman sews. A nurse, aghast,
pretends not to perceive the dog beneath
the patient's bed. Outside, the German troops
(a group of saboteurs who've moved unseen
for months) cut lines to telephones, unsheathe
thin blades and, silent, cinch a metal noose
around each sentry's throat to stifle screams.

German Soldiers Practicing Formations with Canvas Tanks: Photograph

Who wouldn't laugh—grown men in uniforms,
in rows, their jackets buttoned to the throat,
their pant legs neatly tucked into their boots,
as three men shoulder on one side (their arms
placed through three canvas holes) a flapping wall,
some type of kite, perhaps, as four white goats
pass through the rows of men, and one man jolts,
surprised to hear the braying, this alarm.
A man is barking orders at the men.
They move together awkwardly, a strange
ballet. The left side of one tank begins
a slow left turn, releasing. Disengaged,
the right side of the tank turns right instead,
the three men laughing, falling on the frame.

Panzer Grenadiers Rush to Open Fire on a Blazing Soviet Farmhouse Where Russian Sharpshooters Have Taken Refuge During the German Advance to Smolensk: Photograph

What huddles in the house now set ablaze,
the flames extending up the A-frame roof
and meeting at the peak, the wood engulfed
and smoking, billowing dark clouds, a haze
of soot, as Germans rise from turrets, gaze
above the armor of their tanks, or stoop
and run, a shuffling gate? They move in groups
of three or four. The roof begins to sway
as, underneath, three men sit (backs to wall)
between a window and the door. They wheeze
through handkerchiefs held to their mouths, or ball
their shirts and try to make a mask. They seize
and shudder. One man breaks the window, draws
his face beside it, for a moment breathes.

A German Engineering Platoon, Wearing Russian Uniforms and Driving Four Captured Russian Trucks, Attempts to Secure the Dvinsk Road Bridge

Already they are on the bridge, these men
waved by the checkpoint, leaping from their trucks
while Russians race to clog the bridge's ends
and open fire. One German driver slumps
against the steering wheel as bullets thump
the chassis, pierce the truck's cloth sides, his face
against the horn, the shrill sound silenced, done
the moment when the engine goes ablaze.
Three German soldiers (dressed as Russians) race
to cut the wired explosives on the bridge
as other Germans kneel and fire, the haze
of smoke around them like a bog. The ridge
beyond the checkpoint trembles. Sirens wail,
as panzers, tilting forward, crest the hill.

Expecting a Transmission with Information about the Invasion, Russian Soldiers Assemble and Instead Receive Agricultural Reports and Instructions for Daily Exercise

You hear the planes before you see them dive
together through the smoke and ash that spread
from buildings, fill the air the way a hive
will swell en masse, a droning wall, instead
of dissipating. Bombs become the heads
of women, sirens, shrieking as they fall,
each shrill voice matching (so it seems) the dead
and dying on the ground, the sounds of all
the voices of the soldiers' wives. A pall
of dust envelopes streets and buildings, clothes
and rubble. Then the voice from Moscow calls
out from a speaker, squawks above the rows
of peasants, soldiers, citizens: "Reach out.
Extend your arms. Bend down, then up, then down…"

Citizens in Minsk Seize a Bottle Factory to Construct Molotov Cocktails

Two women, kneeling in a window frame,
their red hair falling forward, bend above
a bottle as the older woman tilts
(to steady it) the bottom of a can
against the table's edge. Her right hand shakes
as if she were a mother pouring milk,
as if the younger woman, fidgeting,
were simply late for lessons, wiping down
the lip before she corks the bottle with
a cloth, then exits through the doorway. Here,
the women stand and light the gas-soaked rag,
as, on the street, the tanks grind forward and
the buildings quake. The bottle turns in air,
a dying star, ablaze and falling fast.

Russian General Ivan B. Boldin Observes a Wealthy Official Fleeing in a Limousine Just Before It Is Strafed by a German Plane

The miracle is that the limousine
would stop at all and open up its doors
to greet the general. Nobody screams.
The mother hugs her husband at the throat.
The daughter leans against the father's coat
as, stammering, the father holds a plant
between his shaking knees and slowly strokes
his daughter's hair. And when the father can't
remember what to say, the driver, hands
on wheel, leans back and tells the general
that death has been unchained, is coming. *Stand
back there,* the driver says. The mother balls
her hand and strikes the driver. *Go,* she brays.
The driver, doing what he must, obeys.

A Polish Worker, on Seeing a Ditch Filled with Bodies Before He Is Shot, Remembers a River from His Childhood

Each night, the living ask themselves, "How will
I die?" The words are never spoken, though
they breathe within all other words and give
them motion, force, the way the hollow bones
of birds grant flight. Beside a river, stones
are lifted from the mud and held between
a young boy's finger and his thumb. The rows
of stones the boy has placed on shore will bleach
and speckle, never hatching, never seen
by anyone except the boy who stacks
them carefully, bends slowly, kneels, the scene
so soon forgotten and the riverbank,
the way the river digs into the land,
becomes a wordless grave of water, sand.

Writing in His Journal, Helmut Schreiber, a German Soldier in the Ukraine, Recalls Mistaking a Peasant's Manure Wagon for a Russian Tank

The first sign of a tank and we pull off
the road and lie down in the ditch behind
our motorcycles. Breathing fast, we sight
our rifles, feel the tightening of stocks
pressed into shoulders, bolts snapped closed. All coughs
are stifled. Whispers cease. Breath stills. We're blind
except for scent and sound, the dust a kind
of wall or wave. One soldier, aiming, drops
down to his chest. I blink to clear my eyes
but nothing changes. Then a whistle, low
and lilting, signals for us not to fire.
The smell of shit encircles us and flows
from man to man. The peasant (lucky, dire,
like Death himself) moves though the scene immune.

Rumors Circulate among German Troops of Beautiful Russian Girls Found Dead after Battle, Their Automatic Weapons Still in Hand

Sometimes the girl is standing by the road,
her hand extended to the Germans, dirt
across their faces, arms, and nothing heard
above the grind of engines, jostled loads
of soldiers in the backs of trucks. *I've come
for you,* she says, the heat of air, her words,
against one soldier's skin so that he turns
his head to find her, stands, and she is gone.
Sometimes, alive, she rises from the field
and moves between the soldiers, touching each
of them, her hand along one's arm, one's chin,
her finger tracing from one's jaw to cheek.
I do not loathe the company of men,
she says, then disappears beyond their reach.

Captured by the Germans, Stalin's Oldest Son, Yakov Djugashvili, Speaks of His Father's Refusal to Negotiate His Release in Exchange for a German POW

I would return to find him even now
and stand above him as he dozes, book
on chest, the wicker lounge on which he took
a nap each evening of my childhood. How,
when waking him, my sisters always bowed,
and, startled, he would sometimes laugh, then hook
an arm around one daughter's waist. The look
he gave to me was different. Anxious, proud,
I held his gaze until he stammered, raised
a fist, or said for me to leave him, find
my mother. I confused all things for love,
learned silence from him as a form of praise.
The Germans here believe I am a prize,
yet even they would swap me if they could.

A 12-Piece German Band Performs in a Ukrainian Village Square Where Soldiers and Citizens Have Gathered: Photograph

The soldiers in the crowd stand stiffly, arms
crossed at the chest. The women, hesitant,
hold children, flowers, or they clasp their hands
together. No one dances, sings. What harm
could come from this—the clarinet, the horns
divided into groups, the bass drum and
the cymbals, soldiers bearing music stands?
The trombone player reaches out to turn
the page as, standing on a wooden crate,
the band conductor holds a white baton—
a cadenced hummingbird that quivers, flits.
The crowd surrounds the band the way that they
will circle gallows here, musicians gone,
when bodies turn like silent chimes in wind.

A Ukrainian Man and Woman Search for a Neighbor Among Corpses: Photograph

The voice with which the living call the dead
is always angry, goading them to rise,
to answer. In Kiev, a woman stands
unmoving, weeping, as her husband strides
between the rows of corpses in a field.
He mutters to himself a neighbor's name,
the neighbor who, when banished, swaying heel
to toe, a staggered drunk, would yell—inflamed
and cursing—for his wife to take him back
as other neighbors, strangers, screeched in teams
and bottles flew from windows. Scarf unwrapped,
he sweated, stamped, called out. His body steamed,
an ox in winter. Nothing but his wife,
the front door opening, would silence him.

Stalin, in a State of Depression and Psychic Collapse, Withdraws

Draw curtains closed then take to bed. Don't speak.
Don't rise to answer knocking at the door.
Don't shave. Don't dress. Forget to bathe. Don't seek
advice. Don't take it. When a message bores
into the room (perhaps a note brought on
a silver tray; a voice, imploring, from
the hall; a telegraph?) just stare beyond
the messenger, his white glove raised, his thumb
beside his cheekbone in a sharp salute.
Remove all clocks, all evidence of time.
Don't think. Be vigilantly slight. Be mute.
Alone, see nothing when you close your eyes.
When darkness comes to you, be night. Disperse
in day. Don't hunger. Waste away. Don't thirst.

II. RUSSIAN RESISTANCE AND
THE FALL OF THE LUGA LINE

Russian Partisans Resist 1

What luck to find two hidden German tanks
surrounded by a grove of trees, the men
at rest, sent back to fill supplies perhaps,
or fix these two machines as lines begin
to form across the country, forking up
to Leningrad and east towards Moscow, east
and south towards Kiev, German army groups
all pushing through like rows and rows of teeth.
But here, there's idleness—one man, his hands
across his chest, leans back and dozes on
the tank; another soldier, stitching, mends
a jacket clumsily. And when they've gone
to sleep, we'll circle them with gasoline,
consider nothing, all, then light the trees.

Russian Partisans Resist 2

A wire, unseen, drawn tight across a road
will catch a German motorcyclist
across the throat and break his windpipe, throw
him from his seat, or (honed, a razor) slit
the skin so quickly that his body stays
erect, still holding to the handlebars,
then falling. Darkness: dynamite is laid
beneath a railroad tie, the site not far
from where the Russian (digging with a knife
to hollow out a space no larger than
a loaf of bread) first met his future wife.
She stumbled stepping from the train; he bent
to take her hand. He's breathing heavy now,
bowed low, his dark blade scraping at the ground.

Camouflage Nets Are Strung over Buildings on the Neva River

To lose oneself becomes a form of faith.
The ballerina takes her place among
the other seamstresses. When nets are hung
across the buildings and cathedrals spaced
along the Neva's banks, the structures fade
in unison the way that winter comes
to Leningrad in sheets of ice and snow.
The roads to home, to work, become a maze—
the man who's walked one route for years, now stands
unsure both of himself and of his way,
his body guessing one street and his mind
the other. What geography expands
in him without routine? What crutch remains?
What thought, forgotten, searches him in kind?

Evacuating the Hermitage Museum

The soldiers loading crates onto the train
are overseen by ministers—of State
Security, of Cultural Affairs,
and of Interior—to intervene
if needed, should a soldier try to glean
some minor piece (a ring, bejeweled lace)
and slip it in his coat, into a case
no larger than a flask. El Grecos lean
against Da Vincis. Rembrandt's *Prodigal*
(at twelve feet long and nine feet wide) is boxed
alone and slid into the final car
before the train's caboose: a flatcar set
up with an anti-aircraft gun. The locks
slide closed, then silence as the train departs.

A Russian Farmer Coming Upon German Paratroopers

They jump in darkness, silhouettes against
a canopy of clouds lit from behind,
as if the moon could be restrained, a light
of reticence—a word implied instead
of spoken. As the farmer walks the fence
line of his property, his wolfhound whines
and paws the ground, then draws in close beside
the farmer, lifts its snout to catch a scent.
The chutes descend, small tremors running through
them as the wind shifts slightly—ripples on
the surface of a pond, or like the course
of veins along the backside of a hand.
The ground draws up. On earth, each man shakes loose
the harness like a dog, sheds silk like skin.

A Citizen Firefighter Surveys Leningrad from a Rooftop

Each night—a pail in hand, a shovel held
across my forearm like a rifle—I
ascended to the roof and searched the sky
for bombers, fighter planes, though nothing fell
to me, to Leningrad, but silence. Homes
were caverns. Streets were riverbeds. No crime.
No merchants in the squares. No sense of time.
Stray dogs in single file ran through the streets.
I knew, of course, that no one could escape
the future. Darkness climbed up after me.
I did not weep. I thought of fire in waves,
it leaping from each roof to roof. It seethed
and swelled. I shook it from my mind. A face—
my father's face—appeared to me, then vanished.

Paper Strips, Pasted on Windows to Help Prevent Shattering During the Bombings, Frequently Were Arranged into Elaborate Scenes

Three howler monkeys sit beneath a palm.
One bears his teeth. One swells his chest. One tilts
his head and screeches like a banshee, calms,
then screeches out again, his voice so shrill
the other monkeys turn to look, then fill
the air with shrieks themselves. The palm tree turns
to paper, stills. The breeze that moves within
the fronds solidifies as glass. The churn
of waves, the driftwood in the sand, disperse
to nothing—rows of tape. One monkey's shriek
is silenced then another's as four birds
(all startled, pulsing separately) release
into the air above the palm, then hold,
two beaks forever open, two beaks closed.

A Worker Speaks of Transporting the White Bull Sculptures from the Leningrad Packing Plant

They come to me in dreams. Like dogs, they paw
the ground, a splintering of sparks on stone
beneath their hooves. They breathe like crosscut saws
drawn back and forth across a trunk, a bone.
Their heavy shoulders turn like gearworks, move
in balance, plates of muscle, skin drawn taut
as sails in wind. At work, I pass alone
between the bulls: flanks cold, no corneas,
just white between their eyelids, like the warped
shell of an egg. A ripple from my throat
into my ribcage spreads my chest apart.
In dreams, their breath distills on winter air.
They snort and circle me. One blinks, a fly
caught in his lashes, buzzing there, alive.

Thirty Thousand Leningraders, Mostly Women, Attempt to Return on Foot After Helping to Fortify the Luga Line

A shovel blade struck stone and through her arms
and shoulders, down the channel of her spine,
some shadow life, some memory, rippled. Tree
roots either split beneath the blade at once
(the way a butcher separates a thigh
bone with a single chop) or else a lone
root splintered, fibrous like a coil of rope.
At night, she slept down in the earth she'd dug
and when she woke she climbed back out, began
again, no jokes of resurrection, graves.
Some girls, too tired to run for cover, fell
(pretending to be dead) down in the road
when strafing planes appeared. Who rose from this?
Which matron pulled the living from the dead?

Colonel Bychevsky, Directing the Construction of the Luga Line, Discusses Where to Place Mines

You must anticipate what men will need,
not only where they're going. Soldiers are
controlled by forces that remain unseen,
as much as orders. They must sleep; stripped bare
of quarters, they will search for shelter, scar
the earth with tanks to find a building full
of stockpiles, fresh supplies, a building where
the soldiers might find rest, where they might pull
down sacks of grain and doze against them, lulled
to sleep against the makeshift mattresses,
a sentry whistling softly at the door,
his lips so dry the sound is like a hiss.
Just rest, the body says, *just close your eyes.*
Surrender here to me at last. There's time.

Colonel Bychevsky, on Being Presented with Paper-Mache Decoys of Guns and Tanks Constructed by the Scenic Artists at the Mariinski Theater

Perhaps, Bychevsky thinks, *perception is*
as hollow as he puts his palms against
a tank and, gingerly, leans in towards it
as if a giant bird might hatch—*Defense*
has come to this. Kuznetsov, shyly, hands
Bychevsky two machine guns. (They both weigh
so little that Bychevsky, scowling, bends
one at the stock, then peels off strands the way,
in youth, he picked at scabs when nervous). *Place*
them in the field and German troops will slow,
if only to discern the truth; display
these on the line, draw back, restring the bow,
Kuznetsov says. *Conduct the Germans. Plan*
your strike. Be ghosts. Be patient, then descend.

A Russian Partisan, Running Through a Field, Removes a Machine Gun from Beside the Body of a Dead German: Photograph

The heat held in the barrel of the gun
still lingers when the Russian partisan
bends down to take the weapon. From a stand
of trees, two other Russians, crouching, run
a jagged line across the clearing, turn
along a low stone wall. Without commands,
they scurry, looking left and right, the land
before them opening beyond the grove
into a field of thigh-high grain that stirs
then settles, stirs again. The German's mouth
is closed. Some type of cloth (an undershirt,
a rag, a handkerchief?) extends around
the German's hand. A makeshift flag perhaps?
Spent shells, like husks, lie scattered on the ground.

The German Offensive to Breach the Luga Line

What wakes? What beast, long undisturbed, now stirs?
The currents through the earth shake timbers. Silt
descends from planks that form the ceiling. Files
slide from a desk. The damp smell of the earth
is like a bone-soaked, sodden dog returned
from plunging headlong in a pond; reviled
and placing paws on strangers' chests, he tilts
his nose and snorts, then drops down to all fours.
Bychevsky wipes the dirt out from his hair
as Mukhin lifts their papers from the floor.
A cup of water trembles and the clear
reflection of Bychevsky's profile turns
back on itself and fractures. What is theirs
to know? Like timid hosts, they eye the door.

Zoya Kosmodemyanskaya Sets Fire to a German Stable

Perhaps she pours a trail of gasoline
across the stable's floor then douses walls,
the thick-beamed doors, the hay that lines each stall,
as horses whinny, ears pricked forward. Steam
releases from one mare's long spine, a sheen
of sweat along her back. Her dark neck falls
then rises as she shakes her head. The hollow
at the base of Zoya's throat draws in.
A muscle quivers from her collarbone
to jaw. The match, now struck, burns quickly toward
her fingers as its ash head droops—a monk
in prayer; a soldier slumping, shot alone.
The slightest breath could snuff the flame. The doors
to each stall quiver. Something paces, stamps.

One Russian Soldier from the People's Volunteer Army Discusses the Enclosing German Army

Each time a shell explodes nearby I feel
as if it's been there all along (submerged
beneath the earth, or built into the boards
of buildings) waiting unequivocally
(a bird perched in the branches of a tree?)
for me. The shockwave of the blast is heard
throughout the body, rippling downward, stored
inside the mind as silence, something freed
and lost perhaps—a half-life shaking out
and leaving me, a lesser husk, behind.
The long hydraulic whine when gun mounts turn
and panzers raise their barrels up like snouts
returns and shudders through me every time
I hear the low throat whistle of a bird.

The Evacuation of Children from Leningrad

The last words that my daughter spoke, that filled
the station (so it seemed to me), a crowd
of other children pulling her, distill
into a common voice, a high-pitched sound
of metal bearing down on rails, of steam
releasing through a signal horn. I speak
to her in darkness, in late summer's gleam
of daylight, in the cavity of weeks
that she's been gone. I conjure her to me
the only way I know—rehearsing all
that I have said, would say, in memory, dreams.
My hope for her is like the wind that pulls
the shutters from their hinges, wordless sound,
lone voice, and I am both the wind and house.

An Aerial View of the German Army Closing Around Leningrad

Like veins around the pupil of an eye.
Like tree rings drawing inward towards a core.
Like fingers closing to a fist. Like days
of idleness where silence slowly bores
you through—the cavity that's left behind.
Each tank is like a stone a soldier lifts
and pockets as a souvenir. Each line
of men resembles stitches. Squadrons shift
in air the way a flock of birds will turn
together on a current. Trenches look
like ripples from the city. Houses burn
and seem like flares, like torches held aloft.
And in the center there is Leningrad—
a lone gear turning, or the moon in shadow.

III. THE BATTLE FOR LENINGRAD

The Battle for Leningrad Begins

The first sign of arrival fills the air
when smoke appears, dark red, like iodine
poured into ethanol, a helix, thick
and turning. What the burning marks is time—
the seasons, warehouses of food consumed
entirely as two women pause and stare.
They've just come from the theater. One folds
a shawl into her pocketbook, her bare
arms pink, still tender from a sunburn. Do
they recognize the change when it begins—
the first turn of the carriage wheel; the bloom
of anger in the chest; the sound, the click
an oar makes sliding in its lock? Or would
it come unseen, a face beneath a hood?

The Air Raids

A line for bread forms quickly, then the men
and women scatter at the sirens, stow
themselves in entryways, at windows bricked
and mortared closed, in trenches cut in rows,
haphazardly, along the avenues.
The three or four times that a trolley halts
along a route and patrons empty out
into the streets, to shelters, sandbagged halls,
become routine—they sway together still,
gaze downward, as if waiting for their stop.
At night, the silence in between the shells
becomes the louder sound, a type of rope
that binds, unseen, the sleepless in their beds.
It feeds. It incubates inside the head.

The Badayev Food Warehouses Burn

One drop of melted sugar on the skin
and it will burn—impossible to rub
or rinse away—until the skin is blistered
with welts that rise as dark as rose petals.
To test the heat of sugar, you begin
by pouring it in water so it turns
to threads or spheres or into caramel
when lifted, cooled and rigid, from the pan.
The lesson here is in the hardening,
not in the blaze. A warehouse burns and night
descends around the fire. Combustion needs
more fuel. The fire draws down itself and brings
a ring of bystanders, all drawn by light,
where molten sugar hardens in the streets.

Accusations

My brother's always at the window, night
on night. He crouches, waves his hand at me
for silence when I try to speak. He sees
the phosphorescent arcs; small shells of light
release and rise against the ash-gray sky.
He startles as if waking from a dream.
He points and whispers names, claims enemies
and traitors dwell within the secret lives
of friends. I tell him *think. Be calm.* He strides
towards me in darkness, clicks his teeth, regards
me from my forehead to my chin. *And what,*
he says, *my brother, might you also hide?*
This room at night is like a cave. His words
pulse awkwardly, flit through the air like bats.

To Protect Their Belongings, Some Leningraders Wear Their Finest Clothes

My husband stands before me as a groom
again, his best suit looser on him now.
I hold his waist, draw hips to my hips. How
a part of me desires to be with him
again as adolescents when I drew
him to me, guided him, the night we found
ourselves alone beneath his father's elm,
the sapling planted at his father's birth.
The moon held lightly in the branches. Leaves
turned slowly overhead, each shuddering
when wind would stir, then still. That night recedes
in me at times until those children seem
unknown, as if they were my own. I breathe,
then shyly dress again within his arms.

Taking Cover Under Railway Cars

The rounded undersides of railway cars
are like the abdomens of ancient beasts.
I lightly place my palms against the steel,
the surface colder than I would have thought.
My hands are doctor's hands, perhaps. Their mark
remains in silt, in dust. The handprints seem
like indentations from inside the train,
a stranger lying over me. Unheard,
the man or woman mirrors me, a twin
diminished, held in isolation. Bombs
fall close enough they shake the ground. The wind
lifts scraps of paper, turns them, as the sounds
of voices, coworkers, lift also with
the wind, each trembling as if from a tomb.

In the Workshops

The first time when I saw a person die
I was a child. My father held my hand
as, huddling together, he and I
stood by my mother's bed, the only sound
our breathing in the winter air, a crown
of exhalations over us. The space
between my mother's words grew long, unwound
in me. I'd learned to lean into that loss,
anticipate it, day on day. A burst
of fire in the factory, a shell
released among us, brings death hastily.
The arbitrary loss is hardest. Held
in place by fear, I focus on routine,
say bombs are accidents, try not to dream.

Bombs Fall Near a Zoo

There is communion of the beasts and so
their bodies sing: an elephant (her gray
chest rising) trumpets on her side, the sound
an otherworldly sound, like stone gates pried
apart. An ape stands vigilant beside
the bodies of three others. Reaching out,
he prods them with his hand, unrolls their fingers
then releases them. He snarls and grunts,
then sits and bows his head, his shoulders slumped.
Four sables slash across the ground, their dark
fur glinting, gone, like minnows in a stream.
The cages of the Pavlov Institute
all howl, the long-doomed choir with windows sewn
into their stomachs, bodies thinned to bone.

A Woman Travels Outside of Leningrad to Attempt to Exchange Vodka and Cigarettes for Food

If I were one of them I would not wish
me well. The voice with which the mother speaks
expands in me the way that ice will swell
around a dock's thin slats and posts then split
the wood like kindling. Twenty years ago
I brought a fur, my mother's opal ring.
Tonight, I pass a pack of cigarettes
into their hands, two vodka bottles, shoes
and socks. This type of currency grows dark
and moldering inside my mind. I take
the forty pounds of field potatoes, place
them in my bag. The weight is like a child,
too large to carry, clutching at my hand,
my arm, as I alone pull hard to leave.

A Student Speaks of the Arrival of Winter

I wake, and it is with me in the bed.
It fills my nose and mouth, my throat, my lungs.
It is a fist around my tendons. Held
within its grasp, my joints crack hard and cringe.
It is a cleaver cutting ribs, each rung
sliced clean. Its form on me is neither male
nor female. Something else. Not wind. Not song.
It is not living, is not dead. How frail
and turned my body feels beneath its weight,
like sea glass burnished smooth on sand. The cold
slows time itself. My heartbeat slows. The trail
of thought, of memory, slows. All motion slows
to stillness in my bed, acknowledgement
that heat is miserly, then fickle, spent.

The Mouse

The urge of hunger, scientists advise,
comes from the mind, not from the stomach. Pangs
will linger even when the stomach is
removed—the phantom of a lost limb's pain.
When hunger, in its shadings, is sustained
for months, the body turns back on itself,
consumes itself. Hallucinations take
most any form—a field mouse on a shelf
perhaps. A woman lifts him by the tail,
his pink feet paddling the air. His small
form arcs up slightly as they churn. She lifts
a finger underneath his chest. His long
face seems to vibrate as he breathes, extends
his throat, his nose, to trace some unknown scent.

Imitation

The eating is like make believe, a game
of imitation—sawdust pressed between
two hands becomes a pancake; soup pots steam
with buttons, leather. Call your mother's name,
and she will search for food for you the same
as every other parent. Hallways teem
with children. Turning as if in a stream,
they rise together, speak together, claim
in unison that love will never save
them. *Love alone,* the river answers back,
the river from a dream, two dreams, two halves,
the mother/father, daughter/son, the track
that runs from mouth to stomach. *Eat. Just eat,*
your mother says, as if the word were fact.

A Pigskin Briefcase Is Converted into Pork Aspic

There was no squealing at his birth, no sound
like train wheels straining on their rails, no rush
of light, no rain. The piglet, blind, moved flush
against his mother. Summer came. He found
the ax-hewn trough and grew. Already bound
in him, the future turned—a curved blade humming
on a whetstone. When the farmer hushed
the pig with tongue clicks, led the pig, full-grown,
to market, neither pig nor farmer paused
at separation. Bills changed hands and soon
the pig was gone to slaughter, hung on claws
and drained. Flame seared his skin. A harvest moon
climbed in the sky as each lone piece was bought:
the liver, snout, both pink cupped ears, the hooves...

To Barter for Food, a Girl Removes Her Deceased Father's Gold Teeth

And what would you bequeath your child? The last
word that you spoke? The air that filled the room?
The first night when she sleeps alone? The bloom
of darkness over her? The voices past
the room's one door? Her hunger rising fast?
What way would she begin? Stand close, bend down
and say your name, one candle raised? The tomb
that holds you here is simple: bed and flask,
iron stove and coal (what little you have left).
You must have told her how to take them, told
her as she cried, your hard thumbs rubbing back
her tears, her breastbone shuddering, each breath
a sob. No child would think of this alone.
It would have been a vow, your final pact.

With Their Grandmother's Assistance, Two Children Hide the Bodies of Their Deceased Parents in the Attic

I feel as if they're lying on the earth,
and I'm the one who's buried under them—
as if they're sleeping on my grave, the sun
on them, and they will stir together, heard
by no one, seen by no one, stepping first
between the attic boards, then climbing down
to us. My brother pulls me close to him.
He does not understand their deaths. He's learned
to mimic what I say and do. In line
at noon we place our parents' ration cards
beside our own. There's order in deceit:
we claim our parents cannot walk; we cry
when we are pressed by strangers. *They're not far,*
I say, and every time my dark heart leaps.

One Man, Claiming that He Received an Extra Food Ration for Helping to Build Grenades, Gives His Daily Food Allowance to His Wife

What long-known truth is central to a lie?
Is truth the seed? The lie the blossom? Or
does something keener, something feral, bind
inside that seed, some need, some gesture born
from greed or selflessness, or both? And do
the words become the things they represent?
Eat this, Christ said, *and think of me. For you,*
the husband whispers to his wife. The list
grows long as love itself transforms, transforms
again. *They know not what they do,* Christ cried.
All words are stone. They're ashes in an urn.
As blood, when spilling from the body, lies—
the blue turned red from oxygen, the surge
back towards the heart that beats, *return, return...*

The Aggressor's Plight

The ground is frozen solid four feet deep
into the earth. It splinters wood. It snaps
the blades off shovels, turns dead men to trees,
turns tanks to monuments, splits stones in half.
How quickly everything will freeze: the oil
in trucks, the grease in guns, the water trapped
in railroad engines. Every warmth recoils
into itself. The German soldiers wrap
themselves in stolen blankets, tablecloths
from Russian houses. Tethered horses pull
at frozen tanks. All gears, machine parts, stop.
The earth tilts on its axis. Darkness falls.
Each breath becomes a blade—slid in, removed.
The scarf wrapped at the throat becomes a noose.

IV. THE ICE ROAD

The Children's Sleds

The sound is like two gates pried back against
their hinges, like a lone, shrill voice, like stoves,
ten thousand kettles shrieking, like the sense
that ice will fissure, split, like splintered bones,
like hammers plunging down on railroad ties.
The city is a common grave—the ground
unyielding, frozen, as two women guide
a sled through Nevsky Prospekt. They are bound
together by the body on the sled,
the child between them, by the sound, the grind
of other sleds, all carrying the dead,
all scraping towards a cemetery lined
with bodies. How the cold will keep them, take
them all—for mercy, for its absence's sake.

The Ice Road across Lake Ladoga

The sight of water underneath the ice,
the way it plumes beneath each horse's step,
the way it seems to darken like a rind,
then thin out unexpectedly, then seep
onto the surface—blood that courses, dries
as skin again—takes form and hardens, breath
itself. The path across the ice must rise
beneath the surface like a vein, no less
than everything, no more. The oxygen
that fills each body lifts the ice—a thought
exhaled, inhaled—as each man takes a step
on faith, on fear, suspended, held aloft,
as if the road had risen to him, hands
beneath each step, as fists on which to stand.

A Stolen Ration Card

There is no power granted with each death.
The only wisdom is the certainty
of law that stolen ration cards will bring
the verdict of the soldiers, passionless,
onto the bearer of the card. The theft
itself is not the central crime. The greed
of anonymity is the misdeed.
The Russian soldiers break their ring to let
the man whom they've surrounded move against
a wall. The bullet, passing through the man,
must lodge itself in something firm. In pairs,
the soldiers search him afterwards, a fence
of legs around him, as his last three breaths
evaporate like chimney smoke in air.

Parachute Flares Are Dropped above Russian Supply Trucks Crossing the Lake at Night: Photograph

Each parachute descending opens like
my mother's hand above a candle flame,
her cupping of its light before her face.
Bent over me, she lingered, gaze inside
the flickering, her worried mouth pursed tight.
In two weeks, when the fever lifted, day
drew me to it. Released from bed, I stayed
beyond her, only coming home at night.
I'd hear her heavy limp outside my door.
The floorboards jumped with every other step,
then silence as she peered into my room
to find me curled and feigning sleep. She'd turn,
and then the sound would start again—the left
foot hard, the right foot sliding like a broom.

One Leningrader Discovers in a Snowdrift the Discarded Heads of a Man, Woman, and Young Girl

The woman likely tied the young girl's braids,
pulled hard on them, her left hand parting curls,
her right hand weaving, holding firm—the whirl
of childhood caught impatiently in reins
and bridle. In that grasp, the daughter brayed
to be released; she squirmed and stamped, the world
beyond her, spinning still. Her words unfurled
into that room as proof of will, as prayer.
When Orpheus, in death, his head adrift
atop the river Hebrus, sang out still,
his body, torn from him, was silent. Sift
your hands into the snow until you feel
them sting the way that silence stings. Don't lift
your gaze, your voice. Bend down in reverence. Kneel.

Through the Ice

The first sound is a whine, a splintering
as tilting ice beneath the truck breaks loose
the way a broken bone will push through flesh.
The truck slides aimlessly, one back wheel freed
and spinning as the truck begins to sink,
rear axel first—an animal confused
the moment of the shot, an elephant
that shudders through its haunches, drops to knees.
The cold is like a blow against the chest,
a fist and vise at once. The driver's hands
work frantically. They move like rats. They grasp
at everything. The truck's two headlights spread
light deeper in the water's darkness, dust
specks glinting in the beams like beads of sand.

The Cannibals

In winter, all is darkness by degree—
the evening is a lesser night, the day
like evening. When the soldier first is seen
he too resides in darkness. Shadows drain
his features, steep his coat, his beard, with grays
and blacks like snow that melts then freezes hard
again. There are no dogs, no cats—no strays
of any kind. The soldier's image starts
the night to slither. Stone walls ripple. Carts,
abandoned, creak in alleyways. The sky
descends. The rustling sound of leaves his heart
makes in his chest is heard by no one. *Fly,*
thrums through his ribcage, *fly,* as walls fall in,
bloom hands that pull him, silent, to their dens.

Losing the Path on Lake Ladoga

There is no road, no lake, no map, just stakes
placed intermittently to mark the course.
The slightest deviation—tapping breaks
to dislodge ice or reaching to the floor
to free a wrench wedged in the pedals—turns
the truck into an animal that slides
at will, into a dead bear spinning, four
legs splayed, his body flush against the ice.
At what point does the driver first surmise
that he is lost? What settles over him,
what enters him, when all paths fade? What flies
into the truck's dark cab, extends its limbs
and binds the driver with its wings and claws,
its curved beak nipping at the driver's jaw?

A Reporter Is Dismissed from His Job at *Leningradskaya Pravda* and Expelled from the Communist Party for Using a Newspaper Car to Transport a Sick Colleague across Lake Ladoga

We set out on the frozen lake alone.
My friend is lying on his side, his knees
pulled to his chest, his body wrapped beneath
our only blanket. As his breath curls out,
I watch him in the rearview mirror. Cold
myself, I've packed the car with newspapers
as insulation under him, the seats,
along the floorboards, in the doors and roof.
The feeling on the lake is that the world
is moving under us, that we are still,
and that the engine of the world grinds gear
to gear, its metal teeth entwined the way
two boars will lock their tusks, or how two hands
will interlace their fingers then let go.

Whom None Command

The women fall together on the stairs,
the black-ice-coated stone, the bodies hard
atop the frozen Neva like stray pairs
of logs unmoving towards a mill, whole cords
of wood stopped motionless. Like swollen boards,
the ice creaks underneath them, strains and cracks
the stone. Two holes cut in the ice have formed
a source for water as the sky retracts
from view and stone walls rise. The light refracts
and forms a kind of tunnel holding all,
the lucky ones who fill their pails, whose tracks
across the Neva's dusting, on its caul
of snow, are missives from the recent and
long-dead—those born, unborn, whom none command.

The Supply Chain Is Established

The rows of trucks, the station on the lake's
far side, appear out of the ice like teeth
along a jawbone. Shifting down, we shake
together with the truck. The brake pads seize
then shudder, slip then grab. I haven't seen
the station in a year, and when I climb
down from the cab, I buckle at the scene.
The rows of trucks unloading flour, lines
of them on one side of the station, wind
like vertebrae. They vibrate like coiled springs
as other trucks refuel, load up and find
the tracks across the lake again. A team
of workers greats us, hands us each a roll
dipped into broth and steaming in the cold.

Professor A.D. Bezzubov Creates a Cure for Scurvy by Extracting Vitamin C from Pine Needles

One slight deficiency deforms the mind,
the body. Sores and welts rise up. Raw gums
bleed out. The remedy, like all things from
the earth, is elemental: oranges, limes
and lemons, any source of vitamins.
And though the body, derelict, consumes
itself, with treatment it will heal its wounds,
a kind of suturing, reversing time.
Since fruit is rare, a Russian scientist
extracts the medicine from pine needles.
Eight factories distill the extract. Bits
of glass are melted down and shaped to vials.
The taste is like ground aspirin. It sifts
down through the body, both pure light and bile.

Two Shoots of Green

From chaos there came order. On the lake,
the line of trucks moved swiftly. Bombings slowed.
The drivers loosened at the wheel. Night flowed
around them, and the snow spread like a wake
out from the ruts that formed the road. No breaks
ran through the line of trucks. They jostled, full
of fuel, supplies. Beside a cast-iron stove,
a woman hummed while slicing cornmeal cakes.
As stew steamed in a pot, the earth-walled room
the men had carved out at the station seemed
to inhale with the woman, with the boy
who manned the stove. A soldier, laughing, leaned
against the wall to show the woman two
birch shoots unfurling there their first green leaves.

Russian Tank Crewmen Accept Chocolate from a First-Aid Worker: Photograph

The young men clad in winter camouflage
lounge on a tank. Their clothes, the snow, are white—
a crew of matching ghosts. One soldier lights
a cigarette. It flares as he inhales.
The conversation of the soldiers trails
from them—it vaporizes—with the sight
of someone coming up the road. The bright
red of her fur-lined coat contrasts the males—
a lone camellia blossom in the snow.
She waves to them, this young girl who's a nurse,
one hand deep in her pocket, fingers rough,
the muscles aching in between her thumb
and forefinger from pulling sleds—a hearse.
The men, like schoolchildren, line up at once.

While Flying First-Aid Supplies from Moscow to Leningrad over Nazi Lines, a Pilot Also Transports the Score of Dmitri Shostakovich's *Symphony No. 7*

The cockpit of the single-engine plane
reverberates as shells explode in air
and flak bursts rise within the clouds like flares
in negative, like charcoal lines conveyed
across white canvas. In the air, the name
of the composer, like a coal, is seared
into the pilot's mind. His shadow tears
across the snow. The markings on the page
mean nothing to him—ink marks, rows and lines.
He almost hears a voice above the thrum
of two propellers, hears her song—the sound
heard only as vibration deep inside
his skull—the song the weeping girl had sung
when handing him the music on the ground.

Russian Engineers Cut German Barbed-Wire Barricades to Clear the Way for Soviet Ski Troops and Cavalry: Photograph

The horses and the men both stamp their feet,
the ski troops leaning forward on their poles,
the horses snorting as their damp coats steam,
their sweat evaporating in the cold.
The engineers work quietly. They lie
down on their backs and lift wire cutters to
each line the way a turtle's beak will rise
beneath the surface of a pond. With few
words spoken, soldiers point and nod, each barbed
wire snip a click. The engineers all breathe
like snipers, counting exhalations. Storm
clouds meet the long horizon in a seam.
Night falls. The Russians, charging on the snow,
appear as gods unbound to earth, as ghosts.

The Dream of Summer

The snow diminishes—an argument
abandoned, slowly first, then rapidly.
The sun pursues an oblong path. It spins
across the sky. It turns both as a dream
and as a symbol. Cabbages throughout
the Summer Gardens sprout where lawns once spread.
Potatoes rise from armaments, and crowds
fill Nevsky Prospekt. Teeth sink into bread.
The warm crust fissures like an eggshell. Dreams.
All dreams. The light a dream. Tobacco smoke
that curls from cigarettes, a dream. Tea steams
in cauldrons as a woman bends to stoke
the growing fire. The dark wood twists and cracks,
transforming in the flames to heat, to ash.